Savannas

Joi Washington

See the rocks on the savanna.

See the dirt on the savanna.

See the water on the savanna.

See the trees on the savanna.

See the grass on the savanna.

See the elephants on the savanna.

See the giraffes on the savanna.

See the zebras on the savanna.

See the rhinos on the savanna.

See the hippos on the savanna.

See the beetle on the savanna.

See the snake on the savanna.

See the deer on the savanna.

See the monkeys on the savanna.

See the cheetahs on the savanna.

See the birds on the savanna.

See the lions on the savanna.

See the people on the savanna.

I can use the first letter sound to match the word to the picture.

monkey

bird

tree

zebra

people